IT'S A PROMISE

HOPE FOR TURBULENT TIMES IN WORD, POEM, AND SONG

ELIZABETH SHEPHERD

With All My Thanks!

There is nothing I can say that will adequately express
my appreciation to a great bunch of friends for their
help in getting this book ready to be printed.

To Brenda for proof reading the manuscript and for
listening and suggesting many good things.

To Juanita for bringing together many pieces and
working all kinds of computerized miracles.

To Jim, whose genius in electronics kept me from
pushing the panic button a number of times.

To Judy for making my songs become real by listening,
then putting the notes on paper.

To JD for his patience as he fine-tuned each into
a professional looking sheet of music.

To my family for understanding
and for giving me the space I needed.

To Sylvia for being available
with know-how and understanding.

Most of all, thanks to my Lord and King for
His willingness to use me in His work.

CONTENTS

FOREWORD

This book happened one special summer. Night would come. Sleep would not. I tossed and turned. My mind threatened to explode with fragmented thought. Dread followed me to the bedroom each evening. One such time, as I sat on the edge of the bed trying to decide whether or not to give sleep a chance. I heard a clear whispered command. "Take your Bible and a notebook and go to the family room."

I wasn't very good with whispers, but, then, I wasn't sleepy, so why not? I gathered the things I needed, and shuffled off to the family room. Within no time, I was caught up in one of the most exciting projects I had ever undertaken. For two weeks I read and wrote my way through half of each night. Then the insomnia ended. I asked a friend to type my notes and add some semblance of order. I laid the results on a corner of my desk, and there it sat—forgotten!

Fall came, and Lawrence, my husband, just did not feel well. "What's the matter?" I asked one evening.

"I just don't feel good, and I'm having awful cramps in my left leg."

Shockwaves of fear radiated through my spine and clogged my throat. Another stopped up artery? I glanced in his direction and saw a reflection of my own emotions in his eyes. We had been here before.

Tests not only confirmed the reality of our fears, but they caused him to be rushed to the hospital. He went through two surgical procedures in less than a week, and still there was blockage, probably in the foot. A third surgery was scheduled. Consultations were held first. Round-the-clock medication followed, so I made a quick trip home for clean clothing and other things we needed.

As I prepared to leave the house, I noticed the results of my summer project on the desk. Automatically, I picked it up and tossed it in my bag.

A friend stopped by just then, and we prayed that the artery would be healed. I thanked God, because He was taking care of the healing process. But the day for surgery came, and "Shep" was wheeled back into the operating room. We lost the battle there. His foot could not be cleaned, and his leg was amputated above the knee.

Why, Lord? Did I not have enough faith? Was I wrong when I told the surgeon to take the leg off? How can one person make such decisions alone? Overwhelmed, I reached into my bag and pulled out the pages I had written during the summer. I knew then that the Lord had planned ahead for these unexpected tough times.

The words penned during the midnight hours were a special blessing in the days that followed, and since that time have been shared with several others who were caught up in the storms of life.

INTRODUCTION

S torms come and go. The clouds gather; the thunder roars. The wind bends mighty trees and sends the dust of the earth reeling in frantic whirlwinds. But each storm ends, and the earth stands cleansed; drenched in the golden glow of the sun.

The words that follow are dedicated to all those who are locked in the grip of life's storms. Is the wind bending you to the ground? Dig in and get ready for the sun. It still is shining up there behind the dark clouds of circumstance. Before you know it you will feel its warmth and see its golden light once more.

There was a time in my own life when I thought God took His people around the mountains and over the rivers. Faith was the magic key to happiness ever after.

I still believe in that magic key of faith, and I am very sure there is nothing God can not do. But I am equally sure that God's children can expect to climb dangerous mountains and experience the stormy seas of life. I also know that the Lord hangs in there with us. Sometimes He has to pull us up a steep slope. Sometimes He has to hold our heads above the deep water, but we develop a tremendous set of spiritual muscles in the doing.

Do not be afraid to climb that mountain! Things will look very different at the top. From that vantage point you will begin to understand why God led you up the slope.

Here is an example. H.G. Spafford, a successful Chicago realtor and a devoted child of God, lost his holdings in the great Chicago fire of 1873. Shortly thereafter his wife and daughters set sail for Europe where the girls were to attend school. Their ship was rammed in the middle of the ocean and sank taking Spafford's daughters and many others to a watery grave.

When word of the tragedy reached him, Spafford made plans to go to his wife in Europe. As he cried out to his Lord about his great loss, God answered with healing words and a hymn which is a standard in numerous song books. That hymn has been an inspiration to many people. It begins with these words. "When peace like a river atten-deth my way, when sorrow like sea billows roll; whatever my lot thou hast taught me to say It is well, it is well with my soul."

No water is too deep to cross, no mountain too high to climb when God is with us. Then, like the Apostle Paul, we can say, "This one thing I do. Forgetting what is behind and straining toward what is ahead, I press on toward the goal to win the prize for which God has called me heavenward in Christ Jesus." Philippians 3:13-14 God will straighten out the tangles in our lives and make the pieces fit. If you do not have a personal relationship with Jesus, go to page 68. Then come back and read the rest of this story.

THE BOW MAKER

The little boy struggled to tie his shoe. He flopped the laces one way then the other. No matter how he twisted the stubborn ends, they came out limp and straight, no bow. His mother smiled sympathetically and knelt beside him. "Let me help," she said and took the tangled strings in her own hands. Within seconds there was a bow, a very strong and proper bow.

There are a lot of shoe laces in life that seem impossible to tie, and there is only one who can put those tangled ends together in a nice solid bow. That one is God. He gladly fits the strings together and asks only one thing of those who are His children; that they put their problems in His hands and let Him tie the bows for them. He says, "Take my yoke upon you and learn from me, for I am gentle and lowly in heart, and you will find rest for your souls. For my yoke is easy and my burden is light." Matthew 11:29-30

For many of us this may be the hardest part. We can not let go. Like Jonah, we refuse to let God lead us where He wants us to be. We don't listen when He tells us what He wants us to do. That is why we end up in a whale's belly; up to our necks in half digested muck and seaweed. Even down there we do not understand why we are in such a ridiculous mess. We wipe the slime off our faces and cry, "Lord, why is this happening? What did I do to deserve such treatment?"

It may not be what *you did*; it may be what *you did not do*. Either way, as long as we just sit there sighing and groaning, we will not be able to shake off the slime life throws on us. Things can get pretty tough in a whale's belly.

Just remember this. When Jonah, who was a prophet of God, quit feeling sorry for himself and asked his Heavenly Father for help, the whale spit him out. It must have felt wonderful when the waves splashed over Jonah and washed away all of the garbage. When he was splashed up on the shore and God's gentle, warm sun dried him off, Jonah must have been filled with joy. He was back in the mainstream of life, ready to go again. Then the Lord repeated His instructions to Jonah, and told him to get over to the city of Nineveh. Needless to say, Jonah went.

No matter how hard it storms, no matter how far the darkness extends, there is light ahead. The answer is in God's word. "Trust in the Lord with all your heart, and lean not on your own under- standing, in all your ways acknowledge Him, and He will direct your paths." Proverbs.3:5

The Lord will see you through. He will stoop down to tie that shoe lace if you will hold still long enough, Then He will lead you through the storm ; giving you His peace as you go.

Jesus said in John 3:28 "I will never leave you nor forsake you." When the strands of life are pulling apart, trust Him.

LORD, TIE THE BOW

W hat a statement of commitment! It means that we are ready to give up the struggle, ready to stick out a foot and let God tie the shoe lace that we cannot tie. It means that we are ready and willing to trust Him. And it also means we will not pull the foot back when He gets ready to take care of the problem.

Many of us think it will be easier to buy a pair of loafers and forget the shoe laces. Our goal is to walk around valleys and bypass mountains. We cannot expect God to pat us on the back and say "Nice job!" if we are running along in our own strength. He will not do it. Nowhere in scripture did God say He will help those who help themselves. Instead, He shows Himself to be a God of power to the powerless, a tower of strength to the faint hearted and the weak.

Allowing God to tie our laces and put order in our lives requires faith. "Without faith it is impossible to please God." [Hebrews 11:6] We must know God well enough to be confident that He can and will take us through by directing us down the path He has set before us.

He says, *"Be still, and know that I am God;* I will be exalted among the nations, I will be exalted in all the earth." Psalms 46:10

Are the strings of your life unraveling? Just stop struggling my friend. Commit yourself to trust God and accept His help. He has the answer and He knows the way.Obviously it is easy to talk about commitment, to say as Peter did, "Even if all are made to stumble because of you, I will never be made to stumble." Matthew 26:33 Peter meant what he said. With heart and soul he believed that he would never desert his leader; even if he had to die with Him. Yet before that long night ended, he denied Jesus three times. Was this a strike-out for Peter? As a Christian leader was he a flop? Not so!

The apostle John, writing to Christians who were going through hard times and were troubled by the words of false teachers, said, "If we confess our sins, He is faithful and just to forgive us our sins and to cleanse us from all unrighteousness." I John 1:9

Peter learned some valuable lessons while traveling the dusty roads of Israel with Jesus; among them that losing the battle does not mean the war is lost and that a mistake will be forgiven if we repent and get back on the right road. As a result, Peter gave God the loose ends of his life and went on to become a great witness and a strong force in God's army.

We all have moments of weakness; everyone makes mistakes. The secret is to repent and turn from error when the Holy Spirit rings an alarm bell in our hearts.

Be quiet before your Lord. Let Him tie that bow, so you can get back in life's race and run it to the end.

Jesus knows how easy it is to waiver; how great the desire to go around instead of through. He knows how tempting it is to ask that the raging storm be turned aside before it hits you head-on.
The Son of God knew that His time on earth was nearly ended. He knew that ahead of Him loomed death on a cross and rejection by nearly everyone around Him. He knew that even God the Father would be forced to turn His face from Him when He took on the job of sin bearer for a Holy God could not look on sin.

Aware that only a few hours separated Him from the horrors of Calvary, Jesus went to the Garden of Gethsemane to pray. He took with Him Peter, and the two sons of Zebedee, James and John. He confided in them, "My soul is exceedingly sorrowful, even to death. Stay here and watch with me." Matthew 26:38

Then He went a little further and, in solitude, knelt to talk to His Father. He fell on His face and prayed "Oh, My Father, if it is possible, let this cup pass from me; nevertheless, not as I will, but as you will." Vs 39

Did He not have enough burdens to bear? Yet, when He returned to the three friends He had asked to help Him pray, they were sound asleep. In sorrow he awakened them and asked, "Could you not watch with me one hour?" Vs 40

Two more times he went away and prayed. Two more times He found His supporters sound asleep. At that moment, knowing that no earthly friend was truly with Him in His anguish, it would have been easy for Him to say "Forget it; it's not worth dealing with the things I know are ahead; the taunts, the jeers, the pain. They will not accept the truth anyway."

But He said none of that. He was God. He had come to an hour that had been anticipated since creation-since time began and He was able to say to His Father "Not as I will, but as you will." Vs 39

Because He made that decision we have this promise, "God so loved the world that He gave His one and only Son that whoever believes in Him shall not perish but have eternal life. John 3:16

AND THE STORM RAGES

*M*aster, *the tempest is raging. The billows are tossing high. The sky is o 'er- shadowed with blackness. No shelter, no help is nigh.* I learned these words years ago. They had little meaning then; just a song called Peace Be Still, which was sung by our junior choir.

You have to go through one of life's tempests before you can understand how Jesus' disciples felt that day. You have to feel that little boat rock and pitch on the stormy Galilean sea before you can understand the fear and anguish that gripped their hearts.

Are you among those who are rocking alone out there in life's little boat? You thought things would be okay if Jesus was with you. Now the storm is getting worse. Is the Master asleep? Does He not care what happens to you? Waves are splashing higher and higher. The boat is tipping more and more, and you cry out, "Lord, where are You?"

I have good news. You may feel alone but Jesus is with you. Even as you read this message he knows what is happening and He does care. Hang on tight. He is riding the waves with you and He will keep your head above water.

Every person, every Christian, experiences stormy seas on this voyage through life. Some people will face more storms than others but none of us can totally avoid tough times. Jesus right-hand men were no exception. They handled their problem just like most storm-battered sailors; they were afraid!

Picture their day. It had been busy and stress-filled. Thousands of people gathered early to see and hear Jesus. They pressed close. Some hoped for healing; some were curious and others came thinking they might find free food. Dutifully, the disciples moved among them, responding to the young, the old, the weak, the rich and poor. When Jesus began to speak and the crowd settled down. The disciples also sat down to listen.

Of one thing they had no doubt, they could trust Jesus. He was a teacher like no other. If they stuck with Him, He would change things. There would be victory instead of defeat. There would be bread on the table.

Now the day was over. Everyone was in a good mood, a trusting mood, when Jesus suggested they get in the boats and row to the other side of the lake. The countryside was mellowed by the softening light of early evening. The lake was smooth as glass and a quiet peace curtained the land. It was a good time for a leisurely row across the calm waters, especially with Jesus in the boat.

It did not upset them when their Master curled up in the bottom of the boat and fell asleep. Most of them were experienced fishermen who felt at home on the Sea of Galilee, so Jesus was left to rest. They were relaxed and at peace.

Without warning things changed. Matthew 8:24 says, "And suddenly a great tempest arose on the sea, so that the boat was covered with waves." The disciples struggled to keep the boat upright. It began to take on water. They choked and sputtered as the angry waves rolled over them. Jesus lay silently in the bottom of the boat and the frantic men called to Him. "Lord, save us! We are sinking." Vs 25

He looked up and said, "Why are you fearful. Oh you of little faith?" Vs 26

Jesus arose and rebuked the winds and the raging waters. Calm returned to the troubled sea. Can't you see the disciples staring at the calm water and the returned sun? They looked at Jesus. They looked at each other, and they began to speak softly among themselves saying, "Who can this be, that even the winds and the sea obey Him?" Vs 27.

For them, the storm was a learning experience. They thought they knew Jesus. They thought they knew themselves. This experience on the water made it clear that they were wrong on both counts.

Jesus is a specialist when it comes to wind and waves. He walks with us through fire and He carries us through floods. He never promised that the sea would remain calm, but He did say, "I will never leave you nor forsake you." Hebrews 13:5

Yet you need to remember that God's promises are conditional. He expects obedience. We cannot spend half of our time wrapped in worldly pleasures; then run to our Heavenly Father when storm clouds race in. How can we do His will if we cannot hear Him? How can we hear Him if we are not familiar with His voice? How can we hang onto His hand if we cannot recognize His touch?

Hebrews 13:5 also tells us what we must do if we want this type of loving relationship with Him. "Let your conduct be without covetousness; be content with such things as you have." If you want His promise that He will never leave us, you must take this advice as well.

No matter how bad the storm seems, your boat will not sink; He will be in it. The winds keep blowing, the waves keep beating, but if Jesus has been invited into the boat, you can be sure that He is there.

He knows about the wind. He knows about the waves and the sea will eventually calm, stilled by the loving Master of all Creation. Like the disciples, you will come through the storm with more wisdom and a deeper, more abiding faith.

Are the winds blowing? Are the waves rocking your boat? "Trust in the Lord with all your heart and lean not on your own understanding.

In all your ways acknowledge Him and He shall direct your paths."
Proverbs 3:5-6

Memorize verses like the ones in this chapter. Make them your anchor in times of stress. They will calm your soul and keep you on course when waves of trouble roll over your head.

This Thing Called Faith

W ithout faith it is impossible to please God. (Hebrews. 11: 6).
God's people live by faith. (Galatians. 2:20)

God's people walk by faith (Romans 4:12). They stand by faith
(Romans. 11:20). They overcome the world by faith (1 John 5:4-5).

In his book, *Faith for the Final Hour*, Hal Lindsey says, "The
issue of faith pervades every aspect of our relationship with God
and our service for Him. Faith is the source of our strength, our
courage, our guidance, and our victory over the world system, the
flesh and the devil."

Faith is the only thing that can keep us steady in the trials and perse-
cution predicted for the last days. Therefore, it is important that we
understand what faith is, and how our faith grows.

Faith is the key that opens the door between God and man. It also is
the key that keeps that door open. Faith has always been the key, even
before Christ came. (Hebrews 11) By faith Abraham. By faith Moses.
By faith David. By faith Rahab. By faith Esther. It goes on and on.

Just what is faith? God does not spell it out in so many words but
He splashes descriptions of faith in about 350 verses throughout the
Bible, and that does not include over 100 "faithfuls" that nestle here
and there. A good place to start may be Hebrews 11:1. "Faith is the
substance of things hoped for, the evidence of things not seen."

Faith is a gift from our God. We receive it when we turn over our
lives to Him and God the Holy Spirit takes over the job of directing
our lives. True faith is completely interwoven with trust (Hebrews

11:27). It was because Moses trusted God that he able to turn his back on pharaoh and march right out of Egypt. God spoke, Moses went and just kept going. He had heard God's message and with his spiritual eyes, he saw God marching with him.

Moses had been listening to God. He knew Him so well that he didn't give it a second thought. It was as natural as breathing. God is God. He is my Father; my one and only Father. He talks to me through His Word. What he says goes. I know what He says, and so I do it.

How do we get to that place? We start at the beginning, the place where man meets God. The place where someone tells us about God the Savior; how he died for our sins.

We admit we need something, Someone. We see how badly sin is messing up our lives. We confess that we are sinners; that we want more out of life. We have been told that Jesus Christ, God's Son, died on a cross so that our sins could be forgiven. We ask forgiveness, we believe we have been forgiven, and faith pops into our lives.

This brings us back to Hebrews II:1. We have believed. We feel the presence of God's Spirit in our lives. This is substance. We begin to talk to Him in prayer. We read His Word. We study it. We learn it. Suddenly He is no longer just an acquaintance. He is a special friend. He is unbelievably real. What happiness we feel! We totally trust Him, and our faith is so real that it feels like we can touch it. We have something so substantial that it becomes clear-cut evidence, and the "things not seen" become real. For the rest of our walk with Him this pattern will happen over and over again.

This God, this special friend, opens His heart and His Word to present us with nuggets of truth: though I walk through the valley... I will fear no evil...surely goodness and mercy will follow me.. I am with you always.

The more we learn of God's Word, the more evidence we have, and that evidence becomes a bridge to the things not yet seen. The more we learn about Him and His way, the more we trust Him. Then the peace that passes all understanding is ours.

Faith is not about moving mountains. It is about knowing mountains can be moved, and will be moved, in God's way and in His time. Faith is walking hand in hand with Him no matter how dark the way seems to be. It is trusting Him, knowing that He will lead us over the mountains, through the rivers, and on to the sun that is shining on the far shores of life. Keep your eyes focused on the final destination and the certainty of forever.

Standing on the Promises

How can we stand on the promises of God? How can we know all of the things that God wants us to know? Early in Hal Lindsey's walk with the Lord he began memorizing God's promises. "I memorized hundreds of Bible promises and started to categorize them in a notebook. This was one of the most important things I ever did. These promises have saved me so many times in so many ways", he writes.

In His Word, the Lord says, "Be diligent to present yourself approved to God, a worker who does not need to be ashamed, rightly dividing the word of truth. II Timothy 2:15 KJV.

The Psalmist wrote "Your word I have hidden in my heart that I might not sin against you." (Psalm 119:11) In verse 105, he says "Your Word is a lamp to my feet and a light to my path."

To illustrate the importance of being guided by God, Lindsey tells how, when he was learning to fly an airplane and reached the point when he was to learn how to fly by instrument, he flew directly into a turbulence. His instructor warned him to fly using the readings on the instrument panel. His sense of balance was deceiving him. He was sure that the plane was going down. *Use the instruments.* He thought the plane was banking.

His fingers fairly itched to make a correction. *Use the instruments.* He let the instruments guide him in spite of his feelings to the contrary. That decision probably saved his life. Once again, trust in the Lord with all your heart and lean not on you own understanding and in all your ways acknowledge Him and He shall direct your paths.

God's Word should be the instrument panel in your life. This world has programmed us to trust our feelings and emotions. As we get to know God's Word, hence our Father himself, we are reprogrammed to trust in the Divine viewpoint. "Then we will begin to look at life, not from the standpoint of natural abilities and talents, but through God's *unlimited power* at work within us," writes Lindsay.

As God's Word grows in us, we grow in Him: we become ready to accept Paul's challenge to the Romans. *I beseech you, by the mercies of God, that you present your bodies a living sacrifice, holy, acceptable to God, which is your reasonable service. And do not be conformed to this world, but be transformed by the renewing of your mind, that you may prove what is that good and acceptable and perfect will of God.* Romans 12:1-2

THROUGH THE FIRE

Your commitment to the Lord Jesus Christ is not a passport to easy living. At times the sailing gets pretty difficult and you wonder why you ever put your boat into such waters. God will not dry up the river, but He will help you guide the boat if you let go of the wheel. Knowing that He is riding with you will make the trip much easier. You may even find yourself in a fiery furnace, but if you do, you can depend on your God to be there with you.

Consider Shadrach, Meshach and Abednego, three young men from Israel who were taken to Babylon when the Chaldeans ransacked their land. These fellows, along with Daniel, were from upper-class families in Israel. In their teens when taken from Jerusalem to Babylonia, they had been taught to respect God as well as obey His commandments.

When they arrived in Babylonia all four were taken to the king's palace where they were trained to serve and live among the elite of the land. King Nebuchadnezzer gave them the finest clothing to wear and gourmet food to eat. They were expected to learn the ways of their new country and live accordingly. But there was a big problem. God had given them strict dietary laws to live by. They had a choice. They could stuff themselves with the rich delicacies the king offered and make everyone happy, or they could obey God, eat their own food and make the king and his court unhappy.

As God has told us to do, they chose to be wise as serpents and gentle as doves. (Matthew 10; 16) Sounds good doesn't it? But just how does it work? They went to King Nebuchadnezzer's chief steward and asked to be fed vegetables and water instead of all the goodies.

This request did not sound good to the stewart as his neck would be on the line if the four Hebrews lost weight and began to look pale and sick. Daniel bargained with him for a 10 day trial. "Then take a look at us and compare our looks with the looks of the other young men."

They made the deal. Can you see the king's steward as he hands out the vegetables and water? He is nervous. He watched them crunch carrots and grain, waiting for circles to appear under their eyes. He looked over the other boys who were eating the rich delicacies. He compared their features and tested their stamina. The Bible says at the end of 10 days the Hebrews appeared "better and fatter in flesh than all the young men who ate the king's delicacies." Thus the steward took away their portion of the delicacies and the wine that they were to drink and gave them the food they wanted to eat.. Daniel 1:15

When the training period was over, the king interviewed all trainees. To his surprise, no one compared with Daniel and his friends. "Therefore, they served before the king." "'In all matters of wisdom and understanding about which the king examined them, he found them ten times better than all the magicians and astrologers who were in his realm." vs 1:18-20

Now, is this a lesson in dietetics? No. It is a lesson about being fear-less-about serving God rather than going along with the crowd, It is a story about taking the narrow way God point us to; even though it makes us stand out and can lead to a trip though a fiery furnace, which is our next encounter with these young men.

Daniel was made ruler over the whole province of Babylon and chief administrator over all the wise men. Shadrach, Mechach and Abednego were selected to watch over the affairs of the province .

If you do now or ever have held a position of authority in the work force, you know this did not make the Babylonian "ladder climbers" very happy. These foreigners had been brought in as captives, and now they held some of the most sought after jobs in the county.

"How can we get rid of them?" The Babylonians asked one another. Some of the ladder climbers got together and decided a smear campaign might work, so they watched the "holier than thou" Hebrews. Yes, they appeared to be doing a good job; working hard and with diligence. But wait a minute! These guys were not keeping the king's religious laws! So the enemy forces went to King Nebechadnezzer and told him in all confidence [and only for his own good] that the Hebrews were not following his orders to fall down and worship the golden idol that the king had made.

They reminded him that such lack of loyalty was to be punished by throwing the guilty parties into the fiery furnace. The king felt betrayed and probably embarrassed. That made him angry. If he wanted to save face there was no choice but to pronounce judgment.

Lots of people, even Christians, use these techniques and use them well. Someone tells your friend about something you *presumably* said.

Your friend is mad, and you have no idea why. Or perhaps you have on a brand new outfit and really feel good about yourself. Along comes a "ladder climber" type who says "That's a nice outfit, but you really look better in shades of green? "

There are those who get "laddered" at the work site, in a social circle, even at church. Someone sees you as a threat. A whisper campaign begins, and soon you feel the furnace flames licking at your feet. You may be a housewife or a businessman. You may be in school. The arena is different, but the players do things the same way.

What is your move? You can give in to the demands of the accusers or you can commit your footsteps to God and let Him show you what to do. You may be thrown into the furnace, but you will be delivered-to a better job, a stronger friendship, more time to carry out your commitments to God. Remember what He said in Proverbs 3:5-6? "Trust in the Lord with all your heart.. in all your ways acknowledge Him, and He will direct your paths."

Now back to the three young Hebrews. What happened to them? Obviously, Nebuchadnezzer was furious. He ordered them straight into the fiery furnace and the heat was so intense that it consumed the soldiers who threw them in. They tumbled down to the bottom of the flaming pit through flames that lashed at them from every side. Hands tied, they could do nothing to help themselves. Fire was below them. Fire was above them. Their situation was bad.

Seated at a point high above them, the king kept watch. Suddenly he jumped to his feet and said to his counselors, "Did we not cast three men bound into the fire, into the midst of the fire?"

"True," they responded.

The king stared into the fire pit and said, "Look, I see four men loose, walking in the midst of the fire. They are not hurt and the form of the fourth is like the Son of God."

Nebuchadnezzer cried out to them, calling them servants of the Most High God, and told them to come out of the fire. When they climbed out, the Bible says that their hair was not even singed, their clothing was not burned and they did not smell of smoke. In fact, the king, who had experienced God's presence more than once, put them back in their jobs, even with promotions. Then he made a decree that "any people, nation, or language which speaks anything amiss against the God of Shadrach, Meshach, and Abednego shall be cut in pieces and their houses shall be made an ash heap." Daniel 3:29

The fire and the flood may engulf you, but don't panic. If you belong to God, He is with you. Romans 8:28 assures us that "All things work together for good to those who love God, to those who are called according to His purpose."

No matter how many problems we are faced with God will keep His promise if we put ourselves in His hands. Joseph is another perfect example. Jealous brothers sold him into slavery, but he made a name for himself {rather, God made a name for Joseph] in Egypt.

Then a scorned woman caused him to land in jail. Days turned into years. Finally, God caused him to be released, just in time to lead the nation of Egypt through seven years of famine.

Joseph's position in Egypt enabled him to keep his father and brothers from starving. They came to the country looking for help and found it in the hands of the brother they had mistreated so many years before.

Did Joseph choose to pay back these fellows who had sold him into hardship and slavery? No. He said, "You meant evil against me, but God meant it for good, in order to bring it about as it is this day, to save many people alive. Now, therefore, do not be afraid; I will provide for you and your little ones" .Genesis 50: 20-21

And he comforted them and spoke kindly to them.

The preceding paragraphs show God's pattern for dealing with those who would throw us into the flames. Read His guidelines in Romans 12:14 and l7-21," Bless those who persecute you; bless and do not curse.. Repay no one evil for evil. If it is possible, as much as depends on you, live peaceably with all men. Beloved, do not avenge yourselves, but rather give place to wrath; for it is written. *Vengeance is Mine, I will repay, says the lord (God).* If your enemy is hungry, feed him. If he is thirsty, give him a drink. For in so doing you will heap coals of fire on his head. Do *not be overcome* by evil, but *overcome evil* with *good.*"

I HAVE THIS PROBLEM

S how me someone without problems, and I will show you someone who is dead. (From a Christian perspective, even some of the dead may be having problems.) But every living person faces problems; some far more than others. A well known author and psychiatrist said that wise people learn not to dread but to welcome problems and their pain.

Problems can make us or break us, crumple us or make us stronger. Keep this in mind and travel with me to visit a man named Job. Here was a man who had big problems. Once his life was happy and fulfilled. Once he basked in the sunshine of affluence. He was a godly man, one who helped others; who put God first in his life. But things change quickly at times, and so it was with Job.

Word arrived that all of his worldly goods had been stolen or lost due to fire. That was bad, but things quickly became worse. Now he was told that all of his children and grandchildren were dead; no one left but him and his wife. Job was overcome; his grief was too great to imagine. Devastate though he was, he still had faith to say, "The Lord gave me everything I have, and they were His to take away." Job 1:21

At this point one might expect God to say Job had passed the test and announce that he would be rewarded for his faithfulness. Wrong! More problems were ahead. God next allowed Satan to afflict Job with painful sores from the soles of his feet to the top of his head.

Now that involves a lot of sore spots and the pain became his constant companion. For perhaps the first time, Job began to question God saying, "Why have you set me as your target so that I am a burden to myself?" 7:20

If Job ever needed friends, this was the time. Sure enough, some friends arrived and they sat quietly, mourning with him for seven days. But the quiet support came to an end when Job opened his mouth and said, in essence, that he wished he never had been born.

They were indeed friends, and they did want to help, but their presence became a burden once they opened their mouths .They began searching for a reason behind the events that were happening, and they all turned the spotlight on Job. He must have sinned. He needed more humility, and he needed to repent. Maybe he had disregarded the wisdom of those wise men who lived before; he certainly must have disobeyed God somehow. They kept on until their pain-ridden companion cried out, "How long will you torment my soul, and break me in pieces with words?" 19:2

Even Job's wife got into the fray. Her words of wisdom were, "Do you still hold fast to your integrity? Curse God and die!" 2:9

As often happens when one is locked in the death grip of pain, depression, and despair, Job's physical world was out of control. If God really existed, where was He?

And that is exactly where Job went in his thinking. He raised his eyes heavenward and cried out "Why do you hide your face, and regard me as your enemy?" 13:24

The telephone line to heaven was dead. Job had found no help from medicine, no help from prayer, and no help from wife and friends. He was as down as any human could be, but he still reached out to the God he had learned to know so well with this promise. "As long as my breath is in me, and I have life within me, and the breath of God in my nostrils, my lips will not speak wickedness, nor my tongue utter deceit." 27:3-4

Surely a statement like this proved his loyalty. Surely it was time for a righteous God to step in and calm the storms that raged around his servant Job. True in part! God did step in, but His message had a strange beginning considering Job's situation. This is how His address began. "Now prepare yourself like a man; I will question you, and you shall answer Me."

Job listened to His Heavenly Father and, without question, did what he was told to do. Then God took him on an awe-inspiring tour of creation. He immersed His servant in the power and order of the universe. He pulled out the checkerboard of time and placed every living creature in its proper square. No detail was omitted. Chapters 38-41.

Then the God of all creation challenged Job. "Who is this who darkens counsel by word *without knowledge.*" 38:2

Awestruck and humbled, Job addressed his God with these words, "I have heard of you by the hearing of the ear, but now my eye sees. Therefore I abhor myself and repent in dust and ashes." Job was healed. Everything he had lost, and more, was restored to him. He had beautiful children and grandchildren, and he lived a long and happy life.

Why have we taken this look at Job? God meets us face-to-face in the storms. When we are boxed in, when we have no place to go, when exhausted and beaten, we finally quit fighting; God steps in and shows His majesty. Job had always been God's man, but his journey through the storm gave him a new perspective that increased his value to the Father in His work.

Problems can make us or break us. The stumbling blocks in our lives can become stepping stones to victory.

Sooner or later God brings us through our own personal storms, and like Job we can say, "I have heard of You by the hearing of the ear, but now my eye sees you." 42:5

The book of Job, just before the book of Psalms, gives us an insight into why all this happened, something Job, as a participant, did not know. If you have never read this book I challenge you to get out your Bible and read Job's story.

IT'S NOT A ROSE GARDEN

Do you ever feel sorry for yourself because life has dealt you lemons? I have. At one such time the words of an old song came to mind. A few of you may remember them. "I beg your pardon. I never promised you a rose garden."

Rose gardens are not the norm in this life. The Apostle Paul was getting along in years when he was ushered into a prison cell and it definitely was not his choice, nor was he surrounded by roses in the damp, lonely Roman jail cell. He wrote to Timothy and said, "At my first defense no one stood with me, but all forsook me. May it not be charged against them, *but the Lord stood with me and strengthened* me."

Remember Job? Did God give him a rose garden to relax in? He did just the opposite. Huddled in sackcloth and ashes, sick and penniless, Job had only the ruins of a once happy life to stare at. Still he was able to say, "For I know that my Redeemer lives." Job 19:25

Life is difficult. You can count on that and you also can count on this: life is difficult for *everyone* at some time or other. God's children are not exempt but they do have an advantage; they have a Savior who is with them in the difficult times.

Annie Johnson Flint was a poetess. She also was an invalid who, in one of her many poems, points out that God never promised us flower-strewn pathways but He did promise strength for the day. Her poetry and her life have inspired countless numbers of readers.

Once we are aware that life is difficult at times; once we understand that all human beings, even God's chosen ones, at times experience spiritual prison walls. Once we understand this, we can relax and go about the business of living, the Lord of Creation at our side.

He shares one of many scriptural truths in Philippians 4:6-7. "Be anxious for nothing, but in everything, by prayer and supplication, with thanksgiving, let your requests be made known to God, and the peace of God, which surpasses all understanding, will guard your hearts and minds through Christ Jesus."

If you have accepted Jesus Christ as your personal Savior, He has said I will never leave you nor forsake you. In dozens of scriptures He speaks of the importance of believing and living by faith. This is an important truth: A healthy Christian life depends on the built-in presence of faith. "Faith comes by hearing, and hearing by the word of God." Romans 10:17. This scripture clearly explains how important it is to read God's word and be involved in Bible study. If your time is limited, try less television, fewer fiction books. Time with God now will enrich your fellowship in eternity.

IF YOU LOOK DOWN

Have you ever stood on the shore of a lake and looked down at the water? The swirling currents move restlessly past your vision. Soon your whole body feels like it is moving, tipping over into the tide. You look up and the dizzying movement stops. Your feet are firmly planted on the solid shoreline. It was an illusion. You just had your eyes fixed on the wrong thing.

I stood at the railing of our pontoon boat as we cruised around the lake one day. I watched the wind-ruffled water splashing below me. Ripples came out from under us in ever-widening circles. Suddenly a prickle of fear ran through me. The boat seemed to be rushing sideways; moving rapidly toward the shore at our side. I almost yelled "Be careful. We are about to run onto the shore."

But just in time, I looked up at my husband behind the wheel, and the feeling was gone. He was making his way straight toward the dam where we wanted to go. Everything was fine until I looked down at the water and sensed once more the impending doom. This time, though, I knew what the problem was.

Not long ago I was walking down the road toward my house as I read newspaper headlines. Bang! My head cracked against a tree branch that had grown to the edge of the road. Twice I did the same thing. Why? I was looking at the wrong thing and I was looking down.

That's life. We look down and see circumstances rising up to meet us, and we get that tipsy feeling. It is unsettling, and because of our limited vision, we find ourselves overwhelmed by doubt and insecurity.

God said He will make our paths straight and He promises that He will never leave us nor forsake us. Hebrews 13:5 He also says "Whatever things you ask in prayer, believing, you will receive." Matthew 21:22

There is one catch. You must be listening to Christ Jesus and walking in the path of righteousness which He has chosen for you. Then whatever you ask in prayer will be asked according to His will and He will answer.

Still, you feel the waves are splashing in your boat. No lights are visible on the shore. You are walled-in by circumstances. You truly know that God and His word do not change, but a lot of unexpected things are happening in your life. "Seek first the kingdom of God and His righteousness, and all these things will be added unto you."

God will keep you on course if that is your goal. He loves His children. "The Lord God is a sun and shield; The Lord will give grace and glory; No good thing will He withhold from those who walk uprightly." Psalm 84:11 "Now this is the confidence that we have in Him, that if we ask anything according to His will, He hears us. And if we know that He hears us, whatever we ask, we know that we have the petitions that we asked of Him." I John 5:14-15

IF YOU LOOK UP

One of the most important lessons to learn on the journey through life is to look up. Do not look down at the water. Do not concentrate on the waves. Keep looking up.

There are definite benefits in looking up. You see the sun and feel its gentle warmth on your face. You can watch the clouds, the stars in their entire splendor and the mountains with their dark unmovable strength.

Something great happened when Peter looked up and reached out his hand to Jesus. He walked on top of the water. But then he looked down and he sank. The Israelites looked up and followed God's pillar of fire to the Holy Land. David, the shepherd boy, looked up and killed the giant, Goliath, with his slingshot.

Later, King David penned in Psalm 121, "I will lift up my eyes to the hills from whence comes my help. My help comes from the Lord who made heaven and earth."

Bible scholars believe this is one of several psalms that were sung by pilgrims on their way to the feasts in Jerusalem, the holy city of God. Oh to go to Jerusalem. Oh to worship in God's holy temple. For pilgrims it was a long, hard journey. The relentless sun baked their skin and the hot sand scorched their feet. Mile after mile they trudged through dust-shrouded nothingness. Then, when it seemed that the path would never end, they saw the mountains surrounding Jerusalem.

The tiredness fell away like a heavy cloak. The holy city was near at last! Their steps quickened and they hurried ahead with the words of Psalm 121 on their lips. "My help comes from the Lord," they sang and the words echoed from hill to hill reaching the gates of that great city.

When an Israelite decided to make the Jerusalem journey, he needed to look beyond the loneliness of the hot desert which he had to cross. Jerusalem was his goal. Jerusalem was all that mattered. Perhaps he sang as he drew closer and closer, "He will not allow (my) foot to be moved. He who keeps Israel shall neither slumber nor sleep."

It was time to rejoice, and the travelers probably reassured one another with more words from this psalm. "The Lord shall preserve you from all evil; He shall preserve your soul. The Lord shall preserve your going out and your coming in from this time forth, and even forevermore."

The heat, the long trip, circumstances in general, must have kept many from reaching Jerusalem. Circumstances keep many from reaching their goals today. But there are countless others who have learned to look up, who ignore the circumstances that surround them and just keep pushing along the trail.

Some time ago there was a professional basketball player who became a favorite for many St. Louis fans. In his day he was named an all-time high scorer, something no one would have expected of him when he was a youth because he was much shorter than the average basketball player. As a kid in junior high he was not only small but his success level was pretty low. Once, when going to an out-of-town game, there was not enough room on the bus. Guess who had to stay home.

This kid never quit trying to score in life. He made a name in basketball, and he went on to become chairman of the board of a major bank. His story is not unique. There are thousands of similar success stories about people who kept looking up, stretching farther; who set their sights above circumstances and made it.

God dropped a special promise in the first verse of Psalm 125. "Those who trust in the Lord are like Mount Zion which cannot be moved, but abides forever."

Always remember. Just like the mountains surround Jerusalem, so the Lord surrounds and protects His people. Look up! Trust in the Lord with all your heart. What will happen? God will direct your path. You will make it to your own Jerusalem.

Put your hand in His hand and follow Him into an exciting future! He has a design for you.

DO NOT NEGLECT
THE GIFT THAT IS IN YOU.
I Timothy 4:14

Although Paul was speaking to Timothy in this scripture, his words reach down through the years to us. God has created us with different strengths and different abilities, each with unique gifts to fulfill a special ministry for Him.

You may be artistic, able to make banners and signs, create crafts and decorations. Does God want you to use your talents in church or Bible School? Do you sew? Can you make curtains or costumes, clothing for the needy? Can you clean a place and make it sparkle? Are you are a carpenter who repairs, remodels or builds, listen to God. He gave you your gift, where does He need you?

If you like children, teach or cook, God may need you in His church. Are you at ease with people and speak well? God needs effective witnesses. He gave you your talents to use for Him. In this next section you will meet people who have a way with words, and music. See how God is using them.

But first, I want to tell you a story about myself and how I misused my God-given gifts. When I was young I sang at a few weddings and in duets and trios during college. After college my path took a detour from God's way.

I married. We decided to get back in church. I sat in three different congregations, often urged by others to join the choir, but I declined. I didn't want to leave my husband alone in the pew. My big excuse, however, was that I needed to be humble about my ability to sing; God had better voices than mine out there.

Eventually, in a church in Texas, God fairly lifted me out of my seat with the help of a persistent congregation, and I sang *How Great Thou Art*.

With many disobedient years behind and lots of missed blessings, I saw His gifts for what they are *Our reasonable service to the One who created them in us*.
No matter who you are, no matter what you do, you are nothing more than a tool created and used by our Lord to do the work He calls you to do.

Jesus described Himself as a servant. In Matthew 20:27 He says, "The Son of man did not come to be served, but to serve, and to give His life a ransom for many."

"We are His workmanship, created in Christ Jesus for good works, which God prepared before hand that we should walk in them. Ephesians 2:10.

Be what He wants you to be so that one day you will hear Him say, "Well done good and faithful servant; you were faithful over a few things, I will make you ruler over many things. Enter into the joy of your Lord." Matthew 25:21.

MEET NORM STOVALL

Norm Stovall is a man who is serious about serving the Lord. He and his wife, Juanita, are fun-loving people who, at the same time, are intent on learning about and growing with the Lord. This is his story about himself and one of the gifts God gave him.

The Lord has been good to me even though I went through most of my life turning my back on Him. I was saved in my later years but looking back I can see how He watched over me, even when my back was turned to Him.

One day, as I was about to do my daily Bible reading, I started thinking about things I needed to do, things in life that were troubling me. At that moment the Lord spoke to me and said, "Why don't you just pray?" Immediately I humbled myself before Him and began to pray. When I did, everything seemed a lot clearer.

I began thinking about all the others who probably were going though the same things. So I thought "Why not remind them what prayer can do". God then gave me the words to *If You Just Pray.*

One night, while reading the Bible and praying, I thought about those I come in contact with who need to know the Lord, and others like me who need to be sharing the good news. As a result, God inspired me to write *They need to know.*

Both poems were inspired by the Lord. I pray that everyone who reads them can find the joy and comfort I feel in serving Him. *God* does listen to our prayers.

IF YOU JUST PRAY

By Norm Stovall

All the things you need to do,
All the things that worry you,
All that troubles you today
Would be taken care of
If you just pray.

If you are burdened with a heavy load,
If you are lost and on the wrong road.
If you look to the Lord there is a way,
There is an answer if you just pray.

If you feel your back is against the wall
If there's no friend that you can call.
Have faith in the Lord today,
All you have to do is pray.

If you have a heavy heart
If fear is with you at the day's start.
For love and comfort I can say
You'll find hope if you just pray.

If you are temped and confused,
If all you try you seem to lose.
If Satan has your life at bay
Then you really need to pray. If
forgiveness is your need, Open your
Bible and start to read.
For the price Jesus did pay
So, for forgiveness you must pray.
Pray without ceasing.

THEY NEED TO KNOW

By Norm Stovall

Did you witness for Him today?
Was there someone you talked to at work or at play?
Maybe they don't know Him or what He can do.
There is someone who can tell them - It's you!

Did the thought come to you to tell about Him?
And then you decided, I won't say it to them.
Then you miss your chance to be a witness,
And they won't know about all his goodness.

He walked the earth for thirty three years,
Healing, teaching, and drying up tears.
Thanks to Jesus we are saved from sin.
What we must do is open our hearts and let him in.

Have trust in the Lord and pray each day, The Holy Spirit will
show you the way.
Faith in the Lord will lift you high, Raise your hands and hearts to
the sky.

Jesus died on the cross for all of us,
To save us from sin if we just trust in Him.
He arose from the grave on the third day,
And that is what you need to say.

So when the Lord tells you to witness for Him, Don't question His
order, but speak up to them.
Tell them of His power and saving grace,
And that they too could someday see His loving face.
They need to know.

MEET EMMA JEAN HOUSE

Emma Jean is now in her seventies, but she is a beloved servant of God who accepted Jesus as her Lord and Master when she was 13. Her whole life has been spent serving Him. She believes the scripture when it says that the greatest gift of all is love and she is able to reach out to many because of Christ's love that is visible within her.

She began playing the piano when she was very young; has been a church pianist throughout her adult years. She also is a soloist. Married in the early fifties, she and her husband were going through rough times but the harder the times, the harder this young housewife prayed and read God's word. Then, with two little ones to care for and a third on the way, Emma Jean sat down one day to talk with her Lord and He gave her the words to *Life's Journey.*

The poem, *God's Time*, was written in the early sixties. She often listened to sermons on the radio, and was stirred by one that touched upon the return of Jesus Christ. Emma Jean began to think about her Savior's return and how important it was for people to know about Him and be ready for His return. She sat down at her table and, in thirty minutes, wrote this testimonial poem.

LIFE'S JOURNEY
By Emma Jean House

As I travel on life's pathway
Many are the trials there.
Sometimes shadows hide the sunlight
Shining once so bright and fair.

Then ahead, I meet the faith sign
In bright letters on a cross.
And the shadows seem to vanish,
Trials and fears become a dross.

On the cross I see my Savior
Who gave His life that I might gain
Eternal life through believing
Only in His precious name.

Farther on, I see more trials
Temptations, snares and trials sore.
But with Christ as my conductor
These will trouble me no more.

For in my heart there's courage
And on my lips a song.
My feet will only travel
With the heaven-bound throng.

And when my journey's ended
And I cross the mystic sea
I pray some souls that I have won
Will be up there with me.

GOD'S TIME

By Emma Jean House

God's time clock is ticking swiftly away,
Eternity soon will begin.
Jesus will come to catch up the saints,
Those who are free from all sin.
The dead in Christ will be raised first,
Then we who are alive.
Together we'll meet Him in the sky,
As a thief He will arrive.

God gave us signs in His blessed Word
To show us His coming is near.
O'be not foolish, but wise, that you
Will be ready when He appears.
One will be taken and one will be left
To remain here on the earth
When God shall pour out His wrath on those
Who have not had a new birth.

Oh, I'm so very thankful that I
Believed, received God's Son
As my own dear precious Savior!
Is this what you have done?

You must receive the Savior
As your Redeemer and Lord
If you escape the judgment of God's
Wrath on this world out-poured.

The pain and death in the world today
Can't possibly compare
With the pain and death men will endure
When the saints are gone "in the air".

AN INVITATION TO SING

I am a woman who can hardly read notes and I certainly can't put them on paper. Yet, because I took God seriously when He gave me *Just Another River*. He has used me to write three other songs as well

It began nearly three years ago. The husband you met in the beginning of this book as he was about to have leg surgery, was now moving rapidly into the difficult stages of Alzheimer's disease. It had taken over our lives slowly and unrecognized. It came out of hiding while we were on a trip to Texas; suddenly I was the decision maker. Shep did not know what to do in most situations.

One day, after we came home, I told him to park in a parking spot while I ran in a store. I stood by helplessly and watched as he drove away, leaving me behind. He no longer could drive and it made him angry. He became incontinent. He needed help with everything he did. One evening, he became ill, was taken to the emergency room and, from there to a nursing home where he remains. A few months later the doctor said his brain could no longer control the muscles that allowed him to wear his leg. I was devastated. Alone in the car, the Lord gave me the first verse and chorus of *Just Another River* and I sang it all the way home. The other songs came at different times and in different ways, but always as a result of listening to God.

Just Another River

Betty Shepherd
Arr: Judy Forbes, JD Reynolds

Just Another River

Is There Time For Him

Betty Shepherd
Arr: Judy Forbes, JD Reynolds

Piano

Bu sy night and bu sy day, not much time to stop and
Like a whirl wind spit ting dust we spin on be cause we
We have choi ces in this world. Ma ny things at us are

pray. Lit tle time to spend with Je sus on my way.
must. and so of ten it's our own plans that we trust.
hurled. Some will of crum ble ve ry quick ly once un furled.

There are pla ces I must be. There are things I need to
Je sus has a bet ter way. Take Him with you ev ery
Pret ty flow ers bloom then fall. Where they bloomed we don't re

see. Then the Lord so gent ly whis pers this to me.
day. He will calm your soul, and then once more He'll say.
call. On ly things we do for Je sus last at all.

Is There Time For Him

God is Still Here

Betty Shepherd
Arr: Judy Forbes, JD Reynolds

God is Still Here

My Heart Sings

Betty Shepherd
Arr: Judy Forbes, JD Reynolds

My Heart Sings

THE LAST CHAPTER PROMISE

The most important promise God ever made is in this chapter. This promise is the key to a meaningful relationship with Him; one that involves an unbelievable sacrifice by His Son, Jesus Christ. God made the promise. Jesus fulfilled it. Here it is.

"God so loved the world that He gave His only begotten Son that whoever believes in Him should not perish but have everlasting life. He who believes in Him is not condemned; but he who does not believe is condemned already, because he has not believed in the name of the only begotten Son of God. **John 3:16/18.**

Why did God send His Son to become part of the human race? Why did that Son, Jesus, willingly give His life on a cross, then rise up from the grave, briefly walk among men, then in clear view of hundreds of people, ascend to heaven? God shares the story through a variety of Bible verses. If you, to your knowledge, have never given your life to Jesus, remember that:

> *All have sinned and fall short of the glory of God.* **Romans 3:23**
> *The wages of sin is death.* **Romans 6:23**
> *There is none righteous, no, not one.* **Romans 3:10**
> *But God sent his Son into the world so that the world through Him might be saved.* **II Corinthians 5:17**

In the Old Testament God gave us a set of laws to follow. His guidelines are sprinkled liberally through the first five books of the Bible and summed up in the ten commandments of Exodus 20. These commandments are like a mirror in which we see ourselves as we really are. Read them. Look at yourself as you do and put a check mark beside each law you feel you have broken. Even one check mark will mean you have broken God' rules and stand before Him as a sinner. They are listed below:

You shall have no other God before me. Vs 3 (Nothing and no one must come before God.)
You shall not make for yourself a carved image. Vs 4 (No image made by man is to be worshipped.)

You shall not take the name of the Lord, your God, in vain. Exodus Vs 7 (Do you use God's name wrongly when you are angry or are trying to make a point?)

Remember the Sabbath Day, to keep it holy. Vs 8 (Are you always in church on Sunday? Is your focus on Him?)

Honor your father and your mother. Vs 12 (Respect and obey them regardless of circumstances.)

You shall not kill. Exodus Vs 13

You shall not commit adultery. Exodus Vs 14 (Physical/emotional involvement with anyone outside of marriage)

You shall not steal. Vs 15 (Not even a pencil or a stamp.)

You shall not bear false witness. Vs 16 (Don't lie!)

You shall not covet. Vs 17 (We are not to envy/want something or someone that belongs to someone else.)

Have you checked anything? Yes? God is sinless and can have no fellowship with sin. But through Jesus, a bridge can be built between you and the Father. We cannot buy fellowship with Him; we cannot earn it by doing good works. The Bible says that Jesus was delivered over to death for our sins and was raised to life for our justification (a term that means vindicated or made right).

Jesus said in John 10: 7 and 9, "I am the door of the sheep. If anyone enters by Me, he will be saved, and go in and out and find pasture." In chapter 10: 27-30 He adds, "My sheep hear My voice, and I know them, and they follow Me. And I give them eternal life, and they shall never perish neither shall anyone snatch them out of My Father's hand. I and My Father are one."

He extends this invitation to each of us. "Behold, I stand at the door and knock. If anyone hears My voice and opens the door, I will come in and dine with him, and he with me." Revelation 3:20

Is He knocking on your heart's door? Then it is time for you to answer. "Everyone who calls on the name of the Lord will be saved" Romans 10:13. This has always been His promise: "To all who received Him, to those who believed in His name, He gave the right to become children of God." (John 1:12) He is ready to welcome you home!

The Bible says, "If you confess with your mouth that Jesus is Lord and believe in your heart that God has raised Him from the dead, you will be saved. It is with your heart that you believe and are justified and it is with your mouth that you confess and are saved. (Rom. 10:9-10).

Ask Him right now to forgive your sins. Tell Him you are sorry and ready to begin walking down His path. He will guide you. His Spirit will help you learn how to walk with Him. If you have asked God to forgive your sins and take over as your Lord and Savior, you have begun the first day of your new life.

Do you have a Bible? Begin reading it daily. Start with the book of John (the fourth book in the New Testament.) Keep a yellow marker with your Bible and highlight verses that seem important to you. If you do not have a Bible, find a Christian bookstore and buy one. My favorite Bibles are the New King James (NKJ) and the New International (NIV) versions.

Do you have a friend who is a genuine Christian, one who has a vital and intimate relationship with Jesus? Ask that person to help you find a church, one that believes the Bible is the inerrant Word of God and accepts Jesus as the sinless Son of God who died for our sins, was buried, and returned to life.

Get in the habit of praying. If you csan, set aside a specific time to read God's Word and pray every day. Try not to let anything interfere with your routine. Prayer is a two-way street. Talk to Him. Thank Him. Ask Him for His help and guidance. Most of all, listen to Him. He will speak to you silently through the Holy Spirit. The Bible will verify the truth and show you what is false. It will teach you all about God's perfect plan for you. Mature Christian friends and your new pastor will be a tremendous help to you, too.

Each day you spend time with Him you will get to know our Lord better. Each day you will grow stronger in your new life. It is important to keep in touch with other Christians. The Bible says that we should not forsake the assembling of ourselves together (Hebrews 10:25). It also says "When two or three are gathered together in My name, I am there in the midst of them. (Matthew 18:20)

God bless you as you begin this new walk. Put your hand in His hand and stay with Him on into eternity. I am praying for those of you who read this book that you will grow in the grace and knowledge of our Lord Jesus Christ. (II Peter 3:18)

Now, go back to the front of the book and continue on your journey.

Printed in the United States
45881LVS00007B/418-1008